To my beautiful wife and wonderful children.
You inspire me every day.

Birds have
TWO FEET

Blue Footed
BOOBY
Boobies get their name
from the Spanish word
"Bobo" Meaning clown, or
foolish. Their blue feet come
from pigment in fish they eat,
much like Flamingos
pink feathers.

Lizards
HAVE FOUR FEET

Flap Necked
CHAMELEON
Flap Necked Chameleons can shoot their tongues the length of their body. Chameleons feet are called "zygodactylous" which means they have two toes on either side.

Beetles & Bugs

have even more feet

Scarab
BEETLE
There are roughly
30,000 species of
Scarab Beetles.
A beetle foot is called
a "Tarsi" and is usually
made up of 2-5
segments

SPIDERS
HAVE EIGHT FEET

JUMPING
SPIDER

Jumping Spiders can be
found on every continent
except Antarctica.
They use their feet
and legs to leap
almost 100 times
their body length.

AND
SNAKES
THEY JUST
HATE FEET

GREEN TREE PYTHON

Snakes have been living without feet since they evolved almost 130 million years ago. Green Tree Pythons can also open their jaws 180 degrees.

FISH

DON'T HAVE FEET

BUT THEY

DON'T USUALLY WALK ON THE GROUND

MUD
SKIPPER

Mudskippers don't breath air like land animals and still have gills, but they can walk on land. Some can even climb trees.

THOSE LONG LITTLE MILLIPEDES
HAVE THE MOST FEET AROUND

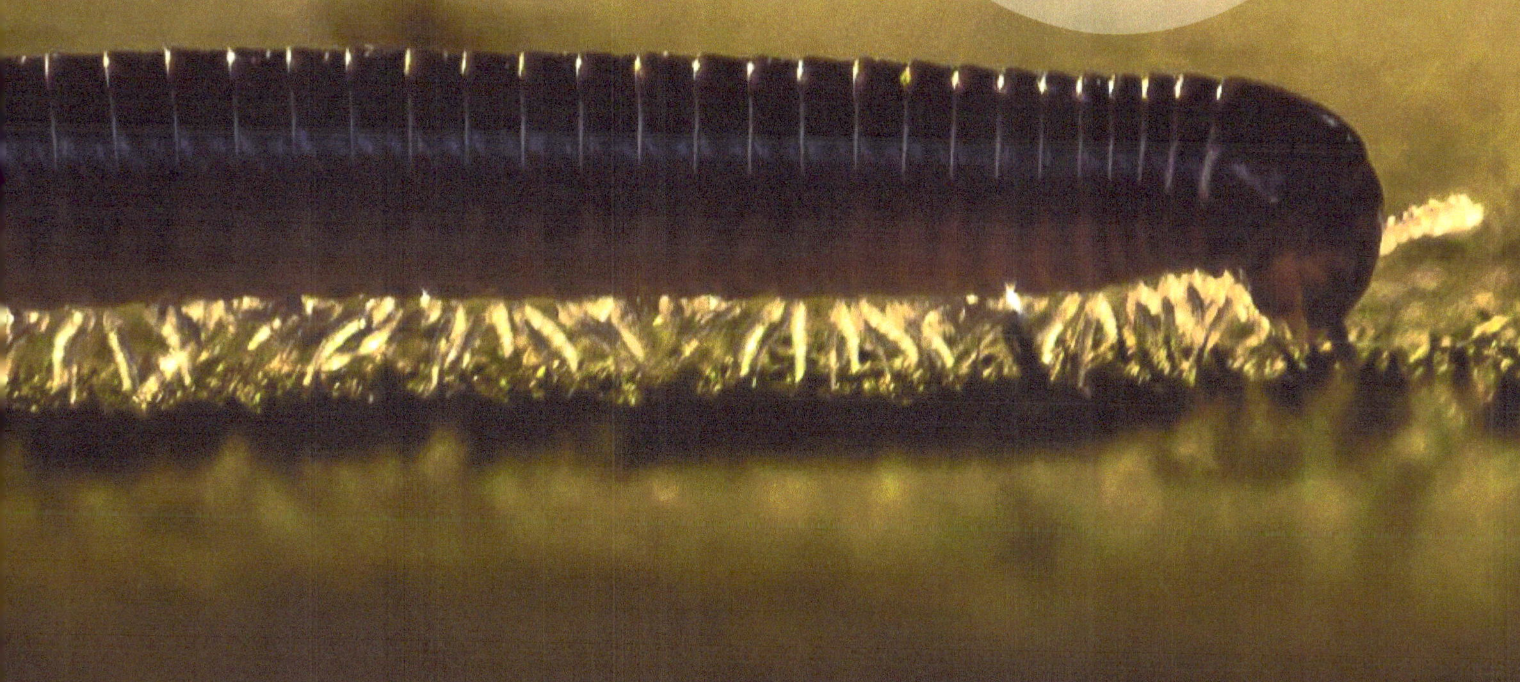

PORTUGUESE MILLIPEDE

Millipedes can have anywhere from 36 to 750 feet. Portuguese millipedes will curl up into a tight spiral when bothered

Horses have hooves

BUT THEY'RE REALLY JUST FEET

Haflinger
HORSE

Haflinger horses have
been around since
medieval times. A horse's
hooves are made of
keratin. The same things
our hair and fingernails
are made of

THE FEET OF ALL CREATURES
ARE REALLY QUITE NEAT

Houston

TOAD

Houston toads are rarely seen animals native to Texas. They can travel around 1 mile in a 24 hour period when foraging for food.

SOME FEET
HAVE TOES
THAT ARE
BIG

SOME FEET
HAVE TOES
THAT ARE
Small

Some Feet
have no toes

SOME FEET
Have claws

SOME FEET
ARE
FAST

CHEETAH
Though considered "big cats" Cheetahs are not closely related to lions, tigers, or leopards. They can run at speeds of up to 75 miles per hour

SOME FEET
ARE
Slow

GALAPAGOS TORTOISE

Galapagos Tortoises
can live up to 175 years
old and have a top
speed
of less than 1 mile
per hour.

All feet are
Special
But some will even
Regrow

Axolotl
Axolotls have the ability to regrow lost or damaged limbs and feet.

Some feet
are not feet.

Some feet
are a foot.

LIKE CLAMS THAT SHUFFLE
in under sea
SOOT

SOMEfeet
ARE SOFT

Some feet
are made
of bones

SOME FEET
ARE SO OLD
THEY'RE NOW
MADE OF STONE

Most People
have two feet

SOME
DO NOT

You sure are

Amazing!

No matter
how many
feet
you've got